Anxiety

The Comprehensive, Straightforward, And Easy-to-follow Step By Step Method To Rewire Your Brain To Fight Stress, Anxiety, And Harmful Thoughts In Both Your Personal And Professional Lives

Richard Manuel Noguera

TABLE OF CONTENT

Cognitive-Behavioural Therapy (Cbt) Strategies Employed In The Treatment Of Social Anxiety . 1

Which Demographic Group Is Most Susceptible To Experiencing Stress? 4

Identifying Automatic Thoughts: 8

The Influence Of Anxiety On An Individual's Life 17

The Identification And Characterization Of Diverse Manifestations Of Intelligence 20

Nurture The Practise Of Gratitude 28

Strategies For Managing And Dealing With Difficult Situations 33

The Impact Of Anxiety On Everyday Functioning 49

What Are The Underlying Factors Contributing To The Development Of Social Anxiety? 61

Indications Of Insecurity And Strategies For Recognising Them 68

Acquiring Fundamental Respiratory Methods 89

The Cultivation Of Self-Compassion Is A Process That Involves Nurturing A Kind And

Understanding Attitude Towards Oneself, Particularly In Times Of Difficulty 93

The Topic Of Interest Pertains To Familial Relationships. 97

Strategies For Stress Management Through Self-Help 104

When Confronted With A Panic Attack, It Is Imperative To Engage In The Process Of Rewiring One's Brain. 117

Effectively Regulate Emotional Responses ... 123

What Is The Recommended Method For Administering Medication? 129

Discovering One's Authentic Identity. The Process Of Emptying Out.! 132

The Potential Hazards Linked To Micro Dosing 136

The Present Discourse Concerns The Topic Of Panic Disorder And Agoraphobia. 139

Cognitive-Behavioural Therapy (Cbt) Strategies Employed In The Treatment Of Social Anxiety

This discourse aims to explore some prevalent cognitive-behavioral therapy (CBT) procedures that can potentially assist individuals in mitigating their social anxiety.

Psychoeducation refers to the process of providing individuals with knowledge and information about mental health conditions

This component is a fundamental aspect of cognitive-behavioral therapy (CBT). Ideally, it is recommended to consider this as the initial step in embarking on one's cognitive-behavioral therapy (CBT) journey. During this phase, the therapist will engage in a process of familiarising themselves with the client, inquiring about their concerns, objectives, and anticipated outcomes for the therapy sessions, as well as their level of engagement and involvement in the therapeutic process. The therapist will also provide an explanation on how Cognitive Behavioural Therapy (CBT) can be beneficial in addressing social anxiety, as well as elucidate the many techniques and approaches that can be employed in the therapeutic process. Consider this scenario as an interactive dialogue aimed at enhancing mutual understanding amongst participants. Ultimately, the efficacy of this therapeutic intervention is contingent upon the quality of the therapeutic alliance established between the individual seeking treatment and their therapist. Please utilise this opportunity to inquire about any inquiries you may have pertaining to the procedure or to provide any pertinent details concerning your medical condition.

The focus of this study is on attention training.

This strategy facilitates the redirection of attention from oneself in social situations. Undoubtedly, individuals with social anxiety encounter difficulties in this regard, as their attention is often directed inward, preoccupied with self-perception and the potential judgements of others. This strategy facilitates the acquisition of skills in active listening and attentiveness towards the behaviours exhibited by individuals during interpersonal exchanges. What is the utility or benefit of this? Recall our previous discourse concerning the potential consequences of excessive self-centeredness, including the tendency to engage in avoidance behaviours and perpetuate social anxiety. This can additionally impede our comprehension of how individuals genuinely perceive us, as opposed to our subjective perception of their perceptions. Attention training has the potential to effectively disrupt the habitual patterns of negative thinking and facilitate the development of genuine interpersonal connections through meaningful engagement with others.

Which Demographic Group Is Most Susceptible To Experiencing Stress?

The level of stress experienced in individuals' lives is heavily influenced by various factors, including but not limited to their physical well-being, the strength of their interpersonal relationships, financial challenges, and other relevant considerations.

Stress manifests in various forms and has an impact on individuals across different age groups and domains of life.

The prediction of stress levels in individuals cannot rely on external criteria. It is not necessary for an individual to have a traditionally demanding occupation in order to experience workplace stress. Similarly, the level of stress associated with parenting may vary between individuals, as a parent with a single child may experience more stress than a parent with numerous children.

The level of stress experienced in individuals' lives is significantly influenced by various personal factors, including their physical well-being, the quality of their interpersonal connections, the extent of their commitments and obligations, the expectations and reliance placed upon them by others, the level of support they receive from their social networks, and the occurrence of recent changes or traumatic events.

Nevertheless, certain factors can amplify our susceptibility to stress or mitigate its severity.

Individuals who possess substantial social support networks, encompassing familial, friendly, religious, or other communal affiliations, tend to have diminished levels of stress and improved mental well-being in comparison to individuals lacking such social connections.

Individuals who experience inadequate nutrition, insufficient sleep, or physical illness may also exhibit reduced abilities to cope with the demands and pressures of daily life, potentially leading to heightened levels of reported stress.

Certain pressures are particularly associated with various age groups or stages of life.

Children, adolescents, young adults, individuals pursuing higher education, individuals balancing work and family responsibilities, and older adults are illustrative instances of demographic groupings that commonly encounter comparable challenges related to various life stages.

Individuals who assume the responsibility of providing care for elderly or infirm family members may also experience a significant amount of stress in their caregiving role.

The presence of a loved one or family member experiencing significant stress often elicits a corresponding increase in our own stress levels.

What are the indicators and consequences of excessive stress or tension that is perceived as being unmanageable?

The manifestations of excessive or inadequately regulated stress might vary significantly.

Numerous individuals assert that stress is associated with the manifestation of various physical and psychological symptoms, such as headaches, sleep disturbances, anxiety, anger, and difficulties in concentration. Conversely, other individuals may express symptoms like sadness, loss of appetite, increased hunger, or a range of other manifestations.

In certain circumstances of heightened severity, individuals may experience an excessive amount of stress that can lead to a state commonly referred to as "burnout," characterised by a diminished inclination towards engaging in customary activities.

Empirical studies have provided evidence indicating that psychological stress has the potential to exacerbate symptoms associated with a wide range of medical conditions.

Identifying Automatic Thoughts:

Automatic thoughts refer to the swift and frequently unconscious cognitive processes that arise in reaction to certain events or stimuli. These cognitive processes are commonly involuntary and have the potential to exacerbate feelings of worry.

The Characteristics of Automatic Thoughts: Automatic thoughts are characterised by their spontaneous nature and their tendency to be imbued with strong emotional content. The aforementioned responses are the first reactions to a given circumstance, frequently indicating cognitive distortions.

In the context of Cognitive Behavioural Therapy (CBT), individuals are instructed to enhance their cognitive awareness by directing their attention towards the automatic thoughts that manifest during periods of anxiety or distress.

The task involves the identification of cognitive patterns that are linked to particular triggers or situations.

Utilising self-monitoring techniques for the purpose of documenting automatic thoughts.

The initial step in questioning and adjusting automatic thoughts is the recognition of their presence, which offers several benefits for anxiety relief. Through the process of recognising these first responses, individuals have the ability to disrupt the cycle of anxiety and substitute automatic negative ideas with more beneficial ones.

Core beliefs refer to deeply rooted and fundamental convictions that individuals hold about themselves, others, and the world. These convictions are frequently established during early stages of development and can exert a substantial influence on the experience of worry.

The identification of core beliefs holds significant importance as they serve as the foundation for automatic thoughts and cognitive distortions. The identification and comprehension of these fundamental beliefs are crucial in order to effectively treat the underlying factors contributing to anxiety.

The function of a therapist in the context of Cognitive Behavioural Therapy (CBT) involves engaging in discourse, inquiry, and guided questioning with individuals in order to reveal their basic beliefs. The identification of these beliefs typically necessitates the establishment of a therapeutic alliance and the provision of a secure environment wherein individuals can freely articulate their thoughts and emotions.

The process of identifying basic beliefs and subsequently working with a therapist to challenge and reframe them offers several advantages in terms of alleviating anxiety. Through the modification of these deeply entrenched beliefs, individuals have the potential to undergo significant and enduring transformations in their cognitive processes and levels of anxiety.

The important steps in the cognitive-behavioral therapy (CBT) process involve the identification of negative thinking patterns, which encompass self-monitoring, cognitive distortion recognition, automatic thought awareness, and core belief exploration. These aforementioned processes facilitate individuals in acquiring a deeper understanding of the underlying causes of their anxiety and devising effective approaches to cope with and ultimately mitigate its influence on their daily functioning.

In the process of introspection and contemplation, individuals engage in extensive cognitive activity. Instead, it is advisable to allocate sufficient time towards the cultivation of our critical and analytical thinking abilities, alongside fostering our intellectual curiosity. However, certain individuals possess a distinct inclination to surpass anticipated outcomes. A well used adage posits that optimal conditions are achieved when phenomena are constrained inside certain boundaries. Here, the aforementioned statement remains valid, and its validity is further reinforced. Individuals who engage in this behaviour often remain oblivious to their unfavourable mental condition until it deteriorates further. The persistent inquiry revolves around the factors that contribute to excessive rumination. What factors might impede our ability to break free from a stagnant state? Individuals who tend to engage in excessive rumination may provide personal testimony on the escalating fatigue and sense of suffocation resulting from their propensity to overthink. Ultimately, they may come to the realisation that the extensive thought they engaged in proved to be entirely futile. Rumination may arise as a consequence of excessive cognitive processing, also known as overthinking, which is widely regarded as an inefficient cognitive strategy. It has been observed that the interference of [the factor being referred to] adversely affects our capacity to manage our emotional responses and sleep patterns, so impeding our ability to derive pleasure from routine activities. Overthinking can be likened to a self-perpetuating cycle. An individual engages in a cognitive process wherein they selectively attend to and amplify negative apprehensions over future occurrences, while also fixating on past experiences. This pattern of behaviour can be characterised as an unhealthy routine that contributes to heightened levels of stress.

It is imperative to introspect and ascertain the underlying reasons for one's current emotional state.

In the event when an individual perceives a state of being overwhelmed by cognitive processes, it is advisable to engage in introspection by posing the question of causality. Could it be attributed to the presence of stress? Do you experience challenges with sleep? Do you get negative emotions on a particular matter? The following inquiries will aid in identifying the origin of one's tendency to engage in excessive rumination.

Is there any unresolved matter that requires attention or resolution?

The act of engaging in excessive rumination does not necessarily have negative implications. The act of engaging in careful consideration prior to reaching a conclusion is inherent to human nature. Individuals who experience a preoccupation with negative thoughts may be exhibiting symptoms of rumination, which is characterised as an unfavourable cognitive process. Rumination refers to the cognitive process of excessively contemplating a particular matter without engaging in corresponding behavioural actions. This mode of thinking has the potential to engender emotions characterised by pessimism, shame, and even sorrow.

Is this an area in which you should strive for improvement?

Occasionally, engaging in excessive cognitive processing may not necessarily yield negative outcomes. Engaging in a process of deliberation prior to reaching a decision is a common and inherent human tendency. Nevertheless, in the event that an individual discovers themselves fixating on negative thoughts, it is plausible that they are partaking in an unfavourable cognitive pattern commonly referred to as rumination. Ruminating can be characterised as an excessive preoccupation with a particular subject or issue, often accompanied by a lack of action or decision-making. This mode of thinking has the potential to evoke emotions such as despair, remorse, and sorrow.

The Influence Of Anxiety On An Individual's Life

The presence of an anxiety condition can have a significant influence on one's daily functioning. The aforementioned factors have the potential to exert an influence on one's interpersonal connections, professional productivity, and holistic state of being. Individuals diagnosed with anxiety disorders often experience difficulties in maintaining focus, making effective judgements, and successfully accomplishing various tasks. Individuals may also encounter physiological manifestations, including but not limited to headaches, abdominal discomfort, and feelings of exhaustion.

fear has the potential to give rise to avoidance behaviours, when individuals deliberately steer clear of circumstances or activities that elicit their fear. This phenomenon has the potential to restrict individuals' prospects for personal advancement and maturation.

Nevertheless, it is crucial to bear in mind that anxiety is a prevalent and manageable condition. The utilisation of mental health professionals has been shown to significantly ameliorate symptoms and facilitate the attainment of a satisfying and meaningful existence for persons.

Understanding Anxiety: Essential Information to Consider

Anxiety is a prevalent mental health problem that impacts a significant number of individuals globally. According to estimates, the prevalence of anxiety is approximately 1 in 13 individuals worldwide. Despite its widespread occurrence, there remains a considerable lack of comprehension among individuals regarding the true nature of anxiety and its potential ramifications on their daily existence.

The manifestations and indications of anxiety

Anxiety has the potential to develop in diverse manners, with symptoms exhibiting variability across individuals.

Several typical physical manifestations of anxiety encompass an accelerated heart rate, muscular tightness, migraines, and sleep disturbances. Conversely, psychological manifestations may encompass heightened levels of anxiety, irrational phobias, and impaired cognitive focus.

The Identification And Characterization Of Diverse Manifestations Of Intelligence

Within the confines of this subsequent , I shall elucidate upon two distinct ideas pertaining to intelligence, which, although certain commonalities in their perspectives, diverge significantly in their consequences. This will elucidate two prominent theories: Howard Gardner's theoretical proposition, which posits the presence of up to seven distinct types of intelligence; and Robert Sternberg's theory of intelligence.

Currently, there exists a lack of consensus on the validity of many theories on intelligence, as I will elucidate shortly. However, each theorist possesses the freedom to advocate for a particular paradigm over another. The objective of this is to present you with the existing data, allowing you to independently arrive at a choice after thoroughly examining the arguments presented in my discourse.

Without any other delay, we commence our discussion with Howard Gardner's theory of Multiple Intelligences.

The seven types of intelligence proposed by Howard Gardner

Howard Gardner, an esteemed American psychologist, is credited with the development of the theory known as "seven forms of intelligence." Occasionally, this theoretical framework is instead referred to as the "theory of multiple intelligences." Gardner posits that intelligence is not a singular thing, but rather comprises multiple "domains" or "forms," as stated in his work. There exists a distinct set of intelligences, specifically seven in number, which can exist autonomously from one another. This implies that an individual may possess exceptional aptitude in one specific domain of intelligence, while exhibiting a lack of proficiency in another. Certain manifestations of intelligence exhibit similarities, whilst others display significant dissimilarities and appear to be disconnected from conventional rational or logical-mathematical intelligence. Let us collectively examine the seven forms of intelligence proposed by Gardner.

Linguistic intelligence, as its name implies, pertains to the aptitude for utilising words and language. Linguistic intelligence is applicable to both written and verbal forms of language. Individuals who possess well-developed linguistic intelligence frequently have a wide-ranging vocabulary and demonstrate a natural aptitude for acquiring new languages. Individuals who possess a high degree of linguistic intelligence often demonstrate aptitude and suitability for occupations such as journalism, writing, interpretation, or translation.

The logical-mathematical intelligence has been previously discussed, and I have no intention of reiterating the principles that have already been presented. Ultimately, it is evident that your inclination towards acquiring further knowledge is apparent. It is important to note that this particular type of intelligence is not solely contingent upon numerical proficiency, but rather encompasses exceptional abilities in abstract reasoning and logical problem-solving.

Spatial intelligence refers to a cognitive capacity that pertains to an individual's aptitude for mentally visualising and comprehending objects and spatial arrangements in three or more dimensions. someone who possess well-developed spatial intelligence demonstrate the capacity to perceive and comprehend intricate information embedded within visual representations or physical environments, which may elude someone lacking such cognitive abilities. Individuals who possess a high level of spatial intelligence have the potential to apply their abilities across a wide range of jobs, including several domains such as military strategy, sports, architecture, and art.

Musical intelligence pertains to the capacity to recognise and generate music. It is likely that you are already familiar with composers that possess the ability to produce creative and intricate musical compositions from a young age, as exemplified by notable figures like Mozart. These individuals, who were indeed children, had evidently not received any formal education in the field of music and composition. They were inherently endowed with exceptional musical intelligence. Individuals that exhibit this particular type of intelligence sometimes possess the additional attribute of possessing perfect pitch, which refers to their innate ability to effortlessly identify frequencies, melodies, and tonalities. Undoubtedly, a vocation in music emerges as an exceptionally fitting choice for individuals with such inclinations. This does not imply that an individual possessing significant musical intelligence is incapable of pursuing opportunities in other domains, such as sound engineering.

The phenomenon of anxiety and insecurity perpetuating one another

Anxious attachment is marked by a recurring pattern of anxiety and feelings of insecurity. The phenomenon under consideration is a self-perpetuating framework of concepts, affective states, and actions that commonly materialises within close interpersonal connections. Comprehending this cycle is of utmost importance for persons who exhibit anxious attachment tendencies and their partners, as it provides insight into the dynamics that can give rise to both emotional turbulence and resilience.

The Inciting Incident: The commencement of the cycle is typically initiated by a triggering event occurring within the partnership. The incident in question can encompass a variety of situations, ranging from a perceived change in the spouse's behaviour, such as delayed responses to text messages, to a real or seen threat to the security of the relationship, such as a partner prioritising time with friends over spending time with the worried individual.

Elevated Anxiety: Individuals with anxious attachment exhibit an increase in anxiety levels in response to a specific triggering event. The primary origins of this anxiety are recurrent emotions of abandonment, rejection, or inadequacy. Manifestations of anxiety may include a heightened state of mental agitation, physiological indicators such as an accelerated heart rate or shallow respiration, and a profound desire for unequivocal reassurance.

Requesting Verification: Individuals with anxious attachment styles exhibit a tendency to actively seek reassurance from their romantic partners due to heightened levels of apprehension. The individual may engage in regular communication via text messages or phone calls, actively seek vocal expressions of affection and commitment, or exhibit behaviours aimed at garnering attention and affirmation.

The experience of relief from confirmation occurs when an individual momentarily has a sense of comfort in response to their spouse providing reassurance or responding positively to their anxious efforts to seek validation. Individuals who are worried may have a decrease in anxiety levels and temporarily find relief from their feelings of insecurity.

The individual experiencing anxiety may develop a reliance on reassurance as a means of managing their anxious feelings. Individuals may develop a reliance on their partner's unwavering affection and assistance in order to experience a sense of security and emotional equilibrium.

Nurture The Practise Of Gratitude.

During periods of heightened worry, individuals often tend to become preoccupied with their issues, so neglecting to acknowledge the positive aspects of their lives. Directing one's attention towards expressions of gratitude serves to displace detrimental cognitive patterns that contribute to the development and perpetuation of worry. Cultivating a habit of expressing thankfulness on a regular basis, even for modest joys, fosters a constructive mental outlook.

Initiate a rudimentary practise of documenting 3-5 elements for which you express gratitude every morning within a personal journal. This establishes a disposition conducive to a day centred around optimism. The purpose of this task is to express appreciation for various aspects and elucidate the associated emotional responses. It is advisable to engage in a contemplation of the existing blessings rather than focusing on perceived deficiencies.

When one becomes aware of the emergence of concerns, it is advisable to revisit past writings in a personal journal as a means of anchoring oneself in a state of appreciation. Occasionally emphasise particularly significant entries to strengthen the overall impact of thankfulness when revisited.

Express gratitude prior to consuming meals, thoroughly relishing each nutritional morsel. Express gratitude for individuals who hold a significant place in one's life and elucidate the reasons behind one's respect for them. It is recommended to express gratitude towards significant individuals in one's life by sending them thank you notes that acknowledge their profound influence.

Demonstrate acts of benevolence by engaging in volunteer work or allocating a portion of one's earnings towards projects that hold personal significance. Assisting others fosters a heightened sense of appreciation for one's own favourable circumstances.

Adopting an attitude of thankfulness can serve as a framework through which one perceives and interprets daily experiences. Even during challenging circumstances, it is advisable to identify and acknowledge a minor aspect that might be valued, such as the presence of a supporting individual, the enjoyment of a preferred dish, or the comforting sensation of sunlight. This straightforward practise cultivates cognitive abilities to identify good aspects.

Now, let us get into a more comprehensive examination of gratitude practises.

• Maintain a gratitude journal in which you record everyday expressions of thanks. It is advisable to review previous entries as a means of obtaining a motivational uplift.

• Engage in the practise of expressing three gratitudes during family gatherings at dinnertime or bedtime, allowing each member to take turns in sharing their appreciations.

Expressing gratitude towards our loved ones by articulating precise reasons for our appreciation is of paramount importance. Engage in the practise of expressing gratitude through the act of sending thank you cards. Additionally, allocate a significant amount of time to fully immerse oneself in the experience of consuming food, allowing for a deep appreciation of each individual sip or bite.

When a positive event occurs, it is advisable to pause and fully experience the sensation of appreciation.

It is advisable to utilise phone reminders to allocate specific moments throughout the day for engaging in a brief period of reflection on appreciation.

One should engage in the practise of reflecting on gratitude before retiring to bed in order to conclude the day on a positive note.

- It is advisable to observe and acknowledge the minor pleasures that occur in your daily life, which are often disregarded.

Expressing thanks towards customer service representatives and baristas is important as pleasant social interactions have been found to build feelings of gratitude.

It is important to acknowledge and value the inherent capacities that are often overlooked or assumed, such as visual perception, auditory reception, locomotion, and respiration.

It is advisable to maintain a continuous record of books, songs, meals, and locations that elicit feelings of thankfulness, with the intention of revisiting them at a later time.

Engage in voluntary activities aligned with a cause that resonates with your personal values in order to cultivate a heightened sense of gratitude towards one's own circumstances.

One should consider sharing their blessings on social media as a means of inspiring others, rather than inciting envy.

Strategies For Managing And Dealing With Difficult Situations

Coping methods play a crucial role in the management and resolution of social anxiety. These tactics enable individuals to effectively address their anxieties, mitigate anxiety, and cultivate self-assurance in social contexts. This section will examine a variety of evidence-based approaches and practises that can assist individuals in effectively managing social anxiety.

1. Cognitive-Behavioral Therapy (CBT): Cognitive-Behavioral Therapy (CBT) is a well-established and efficacious therapy modality utilised for the treatment of social anxiety disorder. The primary objective of this intervention is to discern and confront detrimental cognitive processes and actions linked to social anxiety. The fundamental elements of Cognitive Behavioural Therapy (CBT) encompass:

The process of cognitive restructuring involves the identification and examination of unreasonable thoughts and beliefs that are known to contribute to the experience of anxiety. Substitute the aforementioned viewpoints with perspectives that are more grounded and impartial.

Exposure therapy involves a systematic and gradual approach to confronting dreaded social circumstances, with the aim of reducing anxiety responses and promoting desensitisation to these triggers. Over a period of time, this process leads to a decrease in anxiety responses and fosters the development of self-assurance.

2. The implementation of mindfulness practises and relaxation techniques has been shown to have a beneficial impact on those experiencing social anxiety symptoms, as they effectively promote a state of tranquilly and alleviate the intensity of such symptoms. It is advisable to integrate the following practises into one's daily routine:

Deep Breathing: Acquire knowledge of deep breathing techniques to effectively regulate the functioning of your nervous system and alleviate physiological manifestations associated with worry.

Progressive Muscle Relaxation (PMR) is a therapeutic approach that entails the utilisation of techniques involving the deliberate contraction and subsequent relaxation of certain muscle groups in order to alleviate physical tension.

The cultivation of mindfulness can be achieved through the practise of meditation, leading to an enhanced state of present-moment awareness and a reduction in anxiety levels.

Yoga for Anxiety: Yoga integrates physical asanas, pranayama techniques, and mindfulness practises, providing a comprehensive methodology for alleviating anxiety.

3. The development of self-confidence plays a crucial role in addressing social anxiety. Confidence can be developed through a variety of methods:

Positive self-talk is replacing self-criticism with affirming and constructive internal dialogue. One should endeavour to challenge any negative beliefs they may hold about themselves and their skills.

Establishing Attainable Objectives: Develop attainable objectives that effectively test your limits to confront your anxiety in a manner that is neither too burdensome nor excessively manageable.

The utilisation of visualisation techniques to envision prosperous social interactions, coupled with the implementation of positive affirmations to enhance one's self-esteem, is recommended.

4. Pharmacotherapy: In certain instances, the administration of medicine as prescribed by a healthcare practitioner may serve as a beneficial complement to therapeutic interventions. Pharmaceutical interventions such as selective serotonin reuptake inhibitors (SSRIs) or benzodiazepines have been found to be effective in mitigating the symptoms associated with social anxiety. It is advisable to seek guidance from a healthcare professional in order to ascertain the suitability of medication for your specific circumstances.

5. Lifestyle Modifications: Implementing alterations to one's lifestyle can yield a substantial influence on the management of social anxiety.

The Relationship between Diet and Exercise: A Review of Current Literature
The use of a nutritious diet and consistent engagement in physical exercise has been shown to have a positive impact on mood enhancement and anxiety reduction. Certain types of diet, such as those abundant in omega-3 fatty acids, possess the potential to exert a beneficial impact on mental well-being.

Sleep hygiene is an essential aspect to consider in order to promote optimal sleep quality, as interruptions in sleep have the potential to worsen symptoms of anxiety. Develop a nocturnal regimen that facilitates the attainment of deep and uninterrupted slumber.

6. Social Skills Training: The acquisition of social skills has been shown to have a positive impact on reducing anxiety levels in social contexts. Please take into account the following dimensions of social skills development:

The topic of discussion pertains to the development and enhancement of communication skills. Enhance your proficiency in initiating and sustaining conversations, engaging in active listening, and articulating thoughts with clarity.

The purpose of assertiveness training is to cultivate the ability to effectively communicate one's needs and boundaries in a confident manner, while avoiding extremes of passivity or aggression.

Non-verbal communication encompasses various aspects such as body language, eye contact, and other non-verbal indicators, which can significantly enhance one's social relationships.

7. Support Groups: Engaging in support groups or partaking in group therapy sessions can offer a secure and nurturing setting to cultivate social skills and exchange personal encounters with individuals who possess a comprehensive understanding of your difficulties.

The aforementioned coping methods are not mutually exclusive, and it is often advantageous to integrate numerous ways in order to develop a comprehensive and individualised plan for effectively managing social anxiety. Collaborating with a mental health practitioner can facilitate the customization of these tactics to suit your individual requirements, as well as offer continuous direction and support during your endeavour to surmount social anxiety.

Interactive Component: S—Identifying Indicators

Self-reflection entails the process of introspectively examining one's symptoms and emotions.

Please locate a serene and cosy environment where you may concentrate without any interruptions.

Engage in a series of deep breaths to achieve a state of inner focus and relaxation.

Retrieve a writing instrument and a sheet of paper, or alternatively, use a digital application designed for the purpose of note-taking on your electronic device.

Please transcribe the following headings:

The three components under consideration are as follows: a) physical sensations, b) thoughts and emotions, and c) behaviours.

Take a brief period of time to engage in introspection over your recent encounters and emotional states. Reflect upon instances that elicited feelings of anxiety or melancholy.

Please document the specific indications and symptoms that you have personally observed in yourself under each respective heading. Please provide a comprehensive and candid response, including specific details. Below are few illustrations to initiate your understanding:

Physical sensations refer to the sensory experiences that are perceived through the body's sensory organs, such as touch, temperature, pain, pressure, and proprioception. These feelings play

One common symptom seen by individuals is an accelerated heart rate or palpitations.

The individual may have symptoms such as dyspnea, diaphoresis or tremors, abdominal discomfort or gastrointestinal disturbances, as well as muscular tension or cephalalgia.

b. Cognitive and affective processes:

The symptoms of the condition include constant anxiety or excessive dread, feeling overwhelmed or unable to relax, persistent melancholy or hopelessness, difficulty concentrating or making decisions, and irritability or mood swings.

c. Behaviours:

One common behaviour observed in individuals is the deliberate avoidance of social events or activities.

The observed manifestations include alterations in appetite or sleep patterns, tendencies towards procrastination or diminished motivation, disengagement from previously enjoyed hobbies or interests, and an escalation in substance consumption or engagement in risky behaviours.

After compiling a comprehensive inventory of your signs and symptoms, it is advisable to engage in a period of introspection regarding their ramifications on various aspects of your daily existence, interpersonal connections, and general state of health.

It is imperative to acknowledge that the ability to identify these indicators is a crucial component in the process of engaging in self-care and actively seeking assistance.

If one is at ease, it is advisable to contemplate the possibility of imparting one's perspectives to a confidant, relative, or mental health practitioner.

Please be advised that the purpose of this activity is to promote self-awareness; however, it should not be considered a substitute for professional diagnosis or therapy. For individuals experiencing symptoms of anxiety or depression, it is crucial to seek guidance from a healthcare expert in order to receive a thorough assessment and appropriate support. The importance of one's well-being cannot be understated, and engaging in the process of comprehending one's experiences is a constructive endeavour that fosters self-compassion and personal development.

Prepare yourself for an immersion into Two. Prepare yourself as we reveal the concealed realm of triggers and their influence on the tempestuous manifestations of anxiety and despair. We will provide you with the necessary resources to recognise and effectively manage these triggers, empowering you with valuable knowledge to overcome the obstacles that lie ahead. Prepare yourself to assume control and navigate your path towards a more comprehensive comprehension of your personal triggers.

The Impact Of Anxiety On Everyday Functioning

Anxiety has the potential to permeate various domains of an individual's life. The phenomenon under consideration exerts influence not alone on the domain of mental well-being, but also extends its effects to physical health, interpersonal connections, occupational performance, and overall subjective well-being. Several common ways in which anxiety can disrupt daily functioning include the following:

• Impaired Concentration: Anxiety can impede an individual's ability to maintain attention and concentration on tasks both in professional and personal settings.

• bodily manifestations: Anxiety frequently manifests in bodily symptoms, such as the onset of headaches, muscular tension, and gastrointestinal discomfort.

Sleep disturbances are commonly experienced by individuals with anxiety

disorders, manifesting as difficulties in falling asleep, staying asleep, or changes in sleep patterns.
- Social Isolation: Individuals experiencing social anxiety may exhibit avoidance behaviours towards social contacts, resulting in a state of isolation and feelings of loneliness.
- Diminished Productivity: Anxiety has the potential to negatively impact productivity and academic performance in work or educational settings.

Challenging the Social Stigma: Anxiety is an often experienced emotional state.

It is crucial to bear in mind that the experience of concern does not indicate a state of inferiority or weakness. The phenomenon under consideration is a ubiquitous aspect of the human condition, affecting individuals across many socio-economic backgrounds. According to the World Health Organisation (WHO), anxiety disorders are prevalent mental health conditions on a global scale.

The destigmatization of anxiety can be achieved through the acknowledgment of its inherent presence within the broader spectrum of human experiences. Taking the initiative to pursue therapy and support for anxiety is a courageous decision aimed at enhancing one's overall well-being and cultivating a more fulfilling existence. In the subsequent s, we shall examine pragmatic strategies and methodologies that individuals of average background might utilise to effectively administer and mitigate anxiety.

Factors and Precipitants of Anxiety

The aetiology and precipitating factors of anxiety can exhibit considerable heterogeneity across individuals. It is imperative to acknowledge that anxiety can arise due to a confluence of factors experienced by individuals. The identification and resolution of fundamental causes and triggers play a pivotal role in effectively managing and surmounting anxiety.

Anxiety can arise from various factors and stimuli, which are commonly recognised as causes and triggers.

The concept of stress refers to the psychological and physiological responses that individuals experience when they perceive a discrepancy between the demands placed upon them and

Stress, a pervasive element of contemporary society, is widely recognised as a primary catalyst and instigator of anxiety, intimately intertwined within the very fabric of our day-to-day lives. Anxiety is not simply a temporary inconvenience, but rather a powerful phenomenon capable of triggering a series of emotional and physiological reactions, ultimately leading to the persistent hold of anxiety.

Fundamentally, stress can be defined as the inherent physiological reaction of the human body to perceived dangers or challenges. During periods of heightened stress, our predecessors relied on the 'fight or flight' response to confront predators or traverse perilous circumstances. In the present day, although our circumstances have shifted from encounters with saber-toothed tigers to the challenges of meeting deadlines and managing financial obligations, our physiological responses remain mostly unchanged.

When stress transitions into a chronic state, it creates an environment conducive for the development of anxiety. The persistent pressures arising from occupational obligations, familial duties, financial difficulties, or the incessant influx of digital data can accumulate, resulting in a prolonged state of stress. This tension may be shown as an increased state of concern, agitation, or discomfort.

Furthermore, it is important to note that stress has the potential to worsen pre-existing anxiety disorders. Individuals with a predisposition to anxiety may experience an exacerbation of their symptoms when confronted with persistent stimuli.

The physiological reaction to stress, characterised by heightened heart rate, shallow respiration, and muscular tension, has the potential to intensify the physical manifestations of anxiety, hence augmenting its perceived intensity.

The coexistence of stress and anxiety renders them formidable companions. The cognitive process of rumination and the emotional state of apprehension, which frequently co-occur with worry, have the potential to induce stress, so establishing a cyclic pattern. The experience of stress can lead to the emergence of anxious cognitions, which, in a reciprocal manner, can intensify the experience of stress.

Acknowledging the significance of stress as both a causative factor and a catalyst for anxiety is crucial. The implementation of several strategies such as relaxation techniques, mindfulness practises, regular exercise, and efficient time management can be crucial in effectively managing stress. These approaches not only provide immediate relief from stress but also act as a protective barrier against the negative impact of worry.

Within the complex realm of anxiety aetiology and triggers, stress emerges as a powerful and influential factor.

This highlights the necessity of adopting a comprehensive methodology towards mental well-being, which recognises the interdependence between our physiological and psychological reactions. By recognising and confronting the influence of stress, individuals can adopt meaningful measures to alleviate the grip of anxiety and recover mastery over their life.

I will enumerate the occurrences that transpire during the session.

1. Investigate the underlying causes of the observed behaviours.

What is the underlying motivation behind human actions and behaviours? Have you ever contemplated? The phenomenon of dishonesty being drawn towards individuals, feelings of anxiety regarding certain matters, and challenges encountered in establishing new social connections. Individuals often engage in repetitive behaviours that consistently result in similar outcomes, however remain unaware of this pattern. Therapeutic interventions facilitate the identification of underlying causes for maladaptive behaviours through the process of reframing automatic behavioural responses.

To alleviate or mitigate a particular condition or situation.

The paramount aspect of engaging in therapy is of utmost significance. It is vital to acknowledge that there exists a qualified expert who is readily available to lend an attentive ear. It is important to bear in mind that there exists a distinction between passive hearing and active listening.

3. Expound upon emotional experiences

It is a prevalent occurrence for individuals to experience the amalgamation of various emotions, resulting in the manifestation of a singular, genuine emotional state. The user's text lacks clarity and coherence. Particularly in instances where an individual is experiencing an anxiety attack, panic attack, or another form of disease. Through therapeutic intervention, the clinician will assist individuals in identifying the source and structuring their emotions gradually, employing a range of approaches.

4. Restoration of self-esteem

Individuals who experience low self-esteem possess an intimate understanding of the detrimental effects associated with the cognitive patterns that arise from this condition. Therapeutic interventions facilitate the process of cognitive reframing, which encompasses various aspects, including the introspective examination of one's inner self and the cultivation of self-affection.

The concept of self is a fundamental aspect of human psychology and philosophy. It refers to the individual's sense of identity, encompassing

Self-knowledge encompasses all aspects of human understanding, in my opinion. Individuals who engage in therapy demonstrate an enhanced self-awareness, as well as an improved ability to effectively manage their own challenges through the cultivation of a harmonious equilibrium between rationality and emotionality. During this phase of heightened self-awareness, individuals attain a state of inner tranquilly.

This scientific discipline possesses the capacity to profoundly alter the narrative of one's life. Permit oneself to undergo the experience. Obtaining novel outcomes is unlikely to occur if one persists in employing identical methodologies.

Hypnotherapy has the potential to assist individuals by providing them with anchors that may be utilised each night during the process of falling asleep. The topic of Hypnosis will be further elucidated in subsequent s.

My neighbour has experienced persistent insomnia over an extended period of time and has observed that his sleep onset typically occurs between the hours of 3:00 and 4:00 in the morning. Subsequent to that period, my sleep patterns resembled those of the general population. Subsequently, he autonomously ascertained that nocturnal labour and diurnal rest yielded superior outcomes.

There also exists a category of individuals, referred to as nocturnal owls, that exhibit nocturnal behaviour by being active during the night and sleeping during the day. Although they are not as prevalent, there are instances when such situations exist, and this possibility cannot be ruled out for your particular circumstance. Irrespective of an individual's preference for diurnal or nocturnal activities, it is advisable to consult an expert in order to ascertain the most effective strategies for managing insomnia or anxiety.

What Are The Underlying Factors Contributing To The Development Of Social Anxiety?

There exist various theoretical frameworks that attempt to elucidate the aetiology of social anxiety disorder. Individuals have unique characteristics, and as a result, they are prone to experiencing distinct stimuli that elicit specific responses. Various factors, including one's upbringing, cultural background, and exposure to traumatic events, can significantly influence individuals. In this discourse, I shall elucidate the prevailing factors contributing to individuals' experience of social anxiety.

Behavioural phenomena

One idea posits that the development of social anxiety disorder in certain individuals may be attributed to earlier experiences. It is widely recognised that when a youngster comes into contact with a hot object, such as an oven door, the experience of pain serves as an instructive mechanism, imparting the lesson that oven doors should be avoided due to their propensity to generate high temperatures and cause physical harm. Likewise, instances of social encounters wherein one experienced feelings of humiliation, embarrassment, or fear may potentially influence subsequent emotional states inside future social contexts. Individuals may experience fear that all experiences will exhibit similar characteristics, leading them to develop avoidance behaviours as a coping mechanism.

Evidently, there are several issues with this theoretical framework. For behavioural psychology to be effective, it is necessary to have a consistent and repeating phenomenon. This implies that repeated exposure to embarrassing events is necessary in order for an individual to associate all social interactions with feelings of unease. While it is conceivable that certain individuals may encounter a disproportionately higher number of socially embarrassing situations compared to others, it would require a significant degree of misfortune for the principles of behavioural psychology to be applicable in this context.

Cognitive processes involving mental deliberation and contemplation.

Another theoretical perspective posits that certain individuals possess a cognitive style that predisposes them to experiencing social anxiety. Individuals experiencing social anxiety often engage in negative self-predictions regarding their performance in social situations, perceiving themselves as likely to underperform. Moreover, they tend to harbour the belief that they are constantly being observed and evaluated by others. Individuals who have social anxiety tend to harbour self-doubt regarding their capacity to effectively assimilate and engage in social situations. They often perceive themselves as uninteresting and hold the belief that their contributions to conversations are undesired by others. Cognitive processes of this nature tend to exacerbate ordinary feelings of anxiety, transforming them into more severe manifestations.

Individuals who exhibit this cognitive tendency are frequently referred to as worrywarts or individuals with a pessimistic outlook. These folks exhibit a tendency to seldom adopt an optimistic perspective and consistently focus on potential negative outcomes. Individuals may vary in their propensity for engaging in this mode of thinking, with some individuals being more inclined towards it than others. However, it is important to note that this cognitive pattern is frequently acquired through learning rather than being inherent or instinctive. This development is indeed positive, as it implies the possibility of effectively retraining one's cognitive processes.

Evolutionary factors may potentially contribute to the development of social anxiety disorder. In order to comprehend this phenomenon, it is important to bear in mind that humans are inherently social beings that derive pleasure from engaging in communal activities. Certain individuals may exhibit a reluctance to acknowledge the potential for causing distress to others, coupled with a desire to avoid rejection. Consequently, the development of social anxiety disorder in such individuals might be attributed to their heightened sensitivity towards unfavourable evaluations. This phenomenon could potentially explain why individuals with social anxiety often engage in behaviours that intentionally provoke others, ultimately resulting in self-inflicted damage over an extended period of time.

The subject matter under consideration pertains to the field of biology.

There is also a proposition that social anxiety disorder may exhibit familial associations. Upon retrospective examination of one's familial lineage, it is plausible to posit that the manifestation of social anxiety in an individual may be influenced by the presence of similar features exhibited by their relatives. Although a robust association has been observed between familial relationships and the prevalence of anxiety disorders, the precise aetiology remains uncertain. It remains unclear if this correlation is primarily attributable to hereditary factors or if it is a consequence of children acquiring anxiety disorders by observing and emulating their parents' symptomatic behaviour. Nevertheless, the influence of genetic composition on levels of social anxiety may be more significant than currently understood. Ongoing research efforts persist in this field.

Dealing with Insecurity

The experience of managing insecurity inside partnerships can be very challenging. Insecurity can manifest in several ways, often remaining unrecognised by individuals, whether it pertains to oneself or one's spouse. Instances arise in which individuals experience self-doubt regarding their capabilities to achieve certain objectives, or harbour a need for their loved ones to exhibit indifference towards their well-being.

Indications Of Insecurity And Strategies For Recognising Them

If a someone consistently engages in the act of reprimanding or assigning blame to their partner for all matters, it would necessitate a jarring realisation. This phenomenon occurs when an individual's ego assumes dominance over their interpersonal relationship, employing deceptive strategies to exert control. Is it ever the case that individuals assume responsibility for their actions? Are you willing to adopt a more open-minded approach and consider alternative perspectives without resorting to blame or accusations towards the other party? The ego may compel individuals to actively pursue and identify faults, while engaging in critical examination of the mistakes made by others. The individual in question exhibits a tendency to engage in behaviours that shift responsibility and engage in critical evaluation of others. Surprisingly, the phenomenon we tend to avoid is often what we ultimately encounter in our interpersonal connections. Failure to assume personal responsibility can result in the manifestation of one's ego, leading to the projection of these unresolved issues onto one's partner.

Engaging in a victim mentality

Is it permissible to assert that one is adopting a victim mentality within the context of their interpersonal relationship? Is it common for individuals to engage in self-comparisons with their romantic partners? Is it accurate to say that you consistently engage in self-deprecating behaviour? A maladaptive sense of self-importance might contribute to the reinforcement of harmful behaviours rather than favourable ones. This phenomenon will result in an excessive allocation of time towards the contemplation and scrutiny of one's faults. If one is engaging in this behaviour, it is undoubtedly an opportune moment to revisit and reassess the dynamics of one's interpersonal connection. You do not possess saintly qualities.

It is imperative to own responsibility for one's contributions and refrain from consistently attributing blame on one's partner.

Experiencing Jealousy

Jealousy, sometimes referred to as the green-eyed monster, consistently lays the groundwork for detrimental conflicts inside a romantic partnership. The ego often exploits individuals' self-esteem and, consequently, their lack of recognition. The establishment of a nurturing relationship is contingent upon the mutual respect and mindfulness exhibited by both parties involved. Love does not engage in the act of comparing, belittling, or criticising, unlike the ego. This phenomenon frequently manifests as a highly dramatic kind of conflict within interpersonal relationships. Individuals who find themselves in an abusive relationship may experience difficulty in terminating the connection owing to the influence of their ego, which can manifest as feelings of envy. What factors are influencing your contemplation of these concepts? Does one's spouse elicit doubts regarding the legitimacy of their relationship? This implies a desire to retrospectively adopt a direct approach in recognising and acknowledging the presence of abuse inside the relationship.

Experiencing Apprehension towards Rejection

This particular sense of apprehension hinders one's progress and ability to achieve personal objectives. When individuals allow fear to impede their actions, they are being unjust to their interpersonal connections. Adopting a cognitive shift in one's perception, rather than succumbing to the debilitating effects of anxiety and unease stemming from one's ego, can serve as a beneficial approach to enhancing self-esteem. Engaging in negative self-talk can potentially reinforce one's ego. It is important to maintain one's own identity and not succumb to the demands of a partner's ego. This frequently deviates from being conducive to good health. The establishment of a healthy and affectionate partnership is contingent upon the presence of reciprocal respect and recognition. In the event that an individual experiences feelings of rejection, it may be advantageous to engage in a process of reassessing the nature of their interpersonal connection.

On the eighteenth day.

The objective for today is to initiate contact with a someone who is visually appealing. The marital or committed relationship status of an individual is inconsequential. The phenomenon of attraction is a genuine aspect of human experience, and as social beings, individuals are prone to experiencing heightened nervousness when initiating contact with those whom they find attractive. There is no obligation to disclose this action to one's partner. Participation in this activity does not guarantee an appearance on the television programme known as "cheaters." The objective is to actively encourage individuals to transcend their internal thoughts and engage with the external world. In any case, initiate contact with this individual and either provide a remark on a particular subject or identify a means to initiate a dialogue. One potential negative outcome is the perception of peculiarity by others, however its significance may be diminished for individuals who are already involved in a romantic partnership. If an individual is not in a romantic relationship, it might be perceived as an indication that the person's current circumstances do not align with an ideal or harmonious partnership. The individual served as a project for personal development purposes.

On the nineteenth day

Allocate sufficient time to systematically arrange and categorise any or all domestic possessions that would benefit from such an endeavour. As previously said, engaging in the act of cleaning and organising has the potential to reduce mental clutter. This assertion holds true, particularly in the context of organisational settings. If one's schedule does not allow for extensive time allocation towards organising, it is recommended to allocate a minimum of 30 minutes to a certain area or many areas. It is recommended to engage in an additional walking session this week to promote physical activity, with the objective of covering a minimum distance of 10 blocks.

Upon returning to one's place of residence, it is recommended to allocate a little period of time, ranging from 10 to 15 minutes, to engage in outdoor activities and appreciate the natural environment. It is advisable to refrain from engaging with media gadgets in order to avoid any distractions. Direct your attention towards the surrounding natural environment and engage in a period of relaxation.

On the twentieth day, individuals are encouraged to visit either a zoological park or a cultural institution such as a museum. It is necessary to embark on an individual exploration and thoroughly observe all available elements. This will facilitate the development of self-comfort in social settings characterised by the presence of individuals and familial groups. Engaging in such an activity individually may perhaps enhance relaxation and enjoyment. Upon returning to one's residence, it is advisable to engage in a session of

meditation, subsequently followed by a warm bath infused with aromatherapy.
The twenty-first day.
You have successfully completed three weeks of challenges. Impressive! Take a moment now to grant yourself respite from the multitude of achievements you have attained throughout the course of this week. I encourage you to venture outside of your residence today and engage in self-indulgence. Please compile a comprehensive inventory of your achievements throughout the course of this week and append them to your esteemed catalogue. At this juncture, it is conceivable that one has become cognizant of the extent of their achievements, thereby serving as a catalyst for more endeavours.

The neurocircuitry in mammals involves several key components. Firstly, the thalamus serves as a central hub for gathering sensory information from various senses. This information is then transmitted to the sensory cortex, which is responsible for decoding and interpreting the sensory input. Subsequently, the sensory cortex integrates and processes the information, preparing it for transmission to other brain regions. Specifically, the hypothalamus receives this processed information and plays

The primary neurobiological structures involved in fear-related events are the amygdalae, which are located posterior to the pituitary gland. Each amygdala serves as a component of the fear learning hardware. These factors are fundamental for the effective adaptation to stress and the deliberate alterations of memory related to emotional learning. In the presence of a perceived threat, the amygdalae facilitate the secretion of chemicals that influence the experience of fear and aggression. Upon the initiation of a response to an escalation in fear or hostility, the amygdalae may trigger the release of hormones inside the body, inducing a state of preparedness in the individual. This state enables them to engage in actions such as movement, running, fighting, and similar responses. The physiological response commonly referred to as the fight-or-flight response, which is regulated by the hypothalamus, a component of the limbic system, is characterised by a cautious reaction. After an individual enters an experimental state, wherein potential dangers are no longer present, the amygdalae transmit this information to the medical prefrontal cortex (mPFC) for storage, a process referred to as memory consolidation.

A subset of the hormones necessary during the fight or flight response encompass epinephrine, which regulates heart rate and digestion while also dilating blood vessels and airways, norepinephrine which elevates heart rate and enhances blood flow to muscles, as well as releases glucose from energy reserves, and cortisol which promotes glucose production, augments circulating neutrophilic leukocytes, and influences calcium levels, among other effects.

Following the occurrence of a fear-inducing event, the amygdalae and hippocampus engage in the process of synaptic plasticity to encode the experience. Stimulating the hippocampus can lead to the individual's recollection of many precise details pertaining to the circumstance. The plasticity and development of memory in the amygdala are facilitated by the activation of neurons within this region. Empirical evidence supports the notion that fear conditioning is associated with synaptic plasticity in the neurons of the parallel amygdalae. At times, this phenomenon gives rise to enduring fear responses, such as posttraumatic stress disorder (PTSD) or a phobia. MRI and fMRI scans have provided evidence indicating that individuals diagnosed with certain diseases such as bipolar or panic disorder exhibit enlarged amygdalae, which are structurally and functionally predisposed to heightened fear responses.

Several cerebral areas, in addition to the amygdalae, have been observed to be activated when individuals are presented with scared vs neutral facial expressions. These structures include the occipitocerebellar regions, specifically the fusiform gyrus and the sub-parietal/predominant temporal gyri. The visual cues of fear are manifested through the eyes, temples, and mouth, which seem to exhibit distinct and autonomous reactions inside the mind. Research conducted by experts from Zurich has found that the hormone oxytocin, which is associated with both stress and sexual activity, has the ability to reduce activity in the brain's fear centre.

The act of delivering a speech or presentation to a live audience is commonly referred to as public speaking.

Public speaking is frequently employed by individuals with the intention of exerting influence and persuasion. It is probable that these individuals possess inherent leadership qualities and have attained a high level of proficiency in the domain of effective communication. This does not imply that individuals do not experience anxiety or nervousness prior to delivering a speech in a public setting. This implies that individuals possess a sense of assurance in their abilities to successfully do the task at hand. To facilitate improvement in your public speaking skills, it will be necessary to enhance your self-assurance in this domain. This analysis examines the potential benefits of acquiring persuasive and influential skills in enhancing one's self-assurance in the context of public speaking.

Proficiency in public speaking necessitates a certain level of adeptness in the domains of influence and persuasion. In the context of leadership characterised by a voting process to determine the leader, the significance of persuasion and influence is heightened. The ability to garner the trust and support of a substantial number of individuals becomes crucial in securing one's position as the chosen leader, based on their values, principles, and objectives. The act of persuasion can be achieved without resorting to falsehoods, as evidenced by the various methods available for detecting dishonesty.

There exist many scenarios in which individuals may aspire to exert influence that do not pertain to voting or possess a political connotation. One may find themselves in a situation where they, as a parent, seek to exert influence on their child's decision-making process, or alternatively, attempt to encourage a friend to adopt a specific course of action. These strategies remain applicable to these types of circumstances as well.

The display of self-assurance in one's stance is of utmost importance in the realm of persuasion. The ability to project confidence is heavily influenced by one's nonverbal communication. Adopting a leadership mindset and behaviour in various contexts enhances one's persuasiveness and credibility, irrespective of intimate acquaintance with others.

Psychotherapy, also known as talk therapy, is a form of treatment that involves the

Psychotherapy is often regarded as the prevailing therapeutic approach for individuals afflicted with borderline personality disorder. Treatment plans are frequently tailored to accommodate the specific requirements of individual patients. Individuals diagnosed with borderline personality disorder (BPD) are recommended to engage in extended periods of psychotherapy to enhance their ability to manage and adapt to their condition more effectively. There exist various psychotherapeutic treatments that sufferers may endure, and the subsequent discourse entails an examination of the diverse forms of psychotherapy treatments accessible to individuals afflicted with this condition.

Mentalization-based treatment (MBT) is a therapeutic approach that focuses on enhancing individuals' capacity for mentalizing, which refers The aforementioned approach can be classified as a form of psychodynamic psychotherapy. This intervention is specifically tailored for those diagnosed with borderline personality disorder. The primary objective of this treatment is to facilitate improvements in the patient's mentalization abilities, so enabling the psychotherapist to effectively engage with the patient's present mental condition. Typically, this method is administered in the form of either individual or group therapy. The primary objective of this specific approach is to foster the patient's establishment of emotional bonds with their peers.

Transference-focused psychotherapy (TFP) is a psychotherapeutic approach that is often conducted on a biweekly basis. The intervention is characterised by a high degree of organisation and was specifically designed to cater to those diagnosed with borderline personality disorder. The objective of this psychotherapeutic approach is to mitigate the occurrence of self-injurious behaviours among patients.

Dialectical behaviour therapy (DBT) is a psychotherapeutic approach that seeks to mitigate the propensity for self-harm, suicidal tendencies, and substance misuse among individuals afflicted with mental disorders.

General psychiatric management (GPM) is an evidence-based psychotherapeutic treatment technique that is utilised for the management of various mental diseases. General psychiatric management encompasses several treatment approaches, such as cognitive behavioural therapy and psychoanalytic object relations therapy.

Schema-focused therapy is an integrative therapeutic approach that is utilised to address a broad range of mental and characterological difficulties, including borderline personality disorder. The treatment approach incorporates several therapeutic approaches and theoretical frameworks, including cognitive behavioural therapy, attachment therapy, and psychoanalytic object relations theory, to address the needs of patients.

The effectiveness of psychotherapy treatment choices is heavily contingent upon the characteristics and responses of the patients. Nevertheless, empirical research suggests that mentalization-based therapy and dialectical behaviour therapy have demonstrated efficacy in the treatment of all subtypes of borderline personality disorder.

However, a notable concern associated with psychotherapy is its extended duration, which can impose a significant financial burden on both the patient and their immediate family. The cost of financing an extended psychotherapeutic intervention for individuals with borderline personality disorder is considerably high. However, numerous researchers are currently engaged in the development of abbreviated treatment alternatives with the aim of enhancing the accessibility of this intervention to a broader population.

Nevertheless, the financial aspect of psychotherapy is not the sole factor contributing to the complexity of this treatment choice. Given that individuals afflicted with this particular ailment experience a profound apprehension of being rejected, it is imperative for psychotherapists to exhibit adaptability in their approach towards addressing the adverse ascriptions expressed by the patient.

Acquiring Fundamental Respiratory Methods

The initial technique to acquire is diaphragmatic breathing. The diaphragm is a skeletal muscle located inferior to the rib cage. The same anatomical structure is employed during the acts of laughter and singing. A reliable indicator of proper breathing technique is the sensation of the diaphragm descending into the abdominal region.

Certain individuals of the female gender exhibit a tendency to engage in the practise of manually compressing their abdominal region in order to create the illusion of a slender and taut appearance, often without realising that they are not effectively utilising their diaphragmatic muscles.

The utilisation of the diaphragm is a crucial factor in the reduction of stress levels, as this specific breathing technique effectively communicates a state of relaxation to the nervous system.

Acquiring the skill of regulating one's respiration can be achieved through the practise of deliberate, extended inhalations at designated intervals within the course of a day. To achieve a sense of equilibrium, it is recommended to maintain equal durations for both inhalation and exhalation, counting up to three during each phase of the breath cycle. It is important to ensure a continuous flow without any interruptions or pauses.

This technique facilitates the individual's awareness of their breathing patterns, ultimately aiding in the cultivation of a state of calmness and inward concentration. This technique is based on the principles of meditation.

An additional method to consider involves assuming a supine position on a mat or bed, placing a pillow beneath the upper thoracic region, and engaging in a breathing exercise characterised by a three-count inhalation followed by a three-count exhalation. Once this skill becomes ingrained, individuals can commence the application of this uncomplicated respiratory method while engaging in ambulation, seated positions, executing domestic tasks, or even during temporary halts at traffic signals.

Developing a Regular Breathing Regimen

Regular daily practise of deep breathing exercises for a duration of no less than 10 to 20 minutes is recommended. Nevertheless, by engaging in this activity for a minimum of one minute every hour, you will observe expedited advantageous outcomes.

It is noteworthy that the mere act of being mindful of one's breath can exert a substantial influence on one's cognitive and affective condition.

Proper respiration confers physiological advantages to the human body. Firstly, it assists in the reduction of acidity levels, thereby promoting a more alkaline state within the body. Consider the following: the presence of chronic acidity inside bodily tissues is likely to contribute to the development of chronic illnesses. Therefore, acquiring knowledge on the proper technique for performing deep breaths could potentially prove beneficial.

The subsequent s will provide instruction on various breathing strategies tailored to specific objectives.

The Cultivation Of Self-Compassion Is A Process That Involves Nurturing A Kind And Understanding Attitude Towards Oneself, Particularly In Times Of Difficulty

Stress is well recognised as a persistent mental health issue. The majority of individuals experience its impact on their life. Failure to effectively manage or regulate stress can have detrimental consequences on one's general daily functioning.

Indeed, there exists a significant body of evidence linking stress to a multitude of psychological and physical ailments. The potential consequences encompass depressive symptoms, cardiovascular ailments such as heart disease and high blood pressure, and in severe cases, the occurrence of stroke. The absence of intervention for stress can have detrimental effects on individuals' well-being and overall quality of life. However, it is important to note that effectively managing stress is ultimately a decision that individuals have the power to make.

This implies that the optimal course of treatment can be obtained from within oneself. This assertion is substantiated by scientific evidence. A group of researchers discovered that self-compassion represents a straightforward approach of mitigating stress. Individuals who maintained a sense of self-love were seen to have lower levels of stress compared to their peers.

Furthermore, individuals who possess self-compassion exhibit traits such as optimism, liveliness, and high levels of energy. The study's participants consisted of individuals who were in their first year of college. The researchers posited that the process of transitioning from high school to college is a significant factor contributing to student stress.

And their assertion was accurate. The result was validated by Professor Peter Crocker, who is one of the co-authors of the paper. According to research findings, the initial year of university education is commonly associated with a significant degree of stress.

First-year college students often encounter numerous challenges while adjusting to their unfamiliar surroundings. According to Crocker, those who are accustomed to achieving excellent academic performance may have a sense of surprise upon encountering lower grades in a university setting. Additionally, they may encounter challenges associated with adjusting to independent living away from their family home. Furthermore, these individuals often find themselves lacking the significant social connections they had established during their high school years.

However, students can effectively manage stress provided they possess the necessary skills to do so. The discovery implies the most straightforward approach to alleviate stress among college students. According to Crocker, self-compassion seems to be a viable approach or asset for managing these particular challenges.

The impact of this study extends beyond the student population. Individuals from many backgrounds and professions can derive advantages from this discovery. Stress frequently arises when an individual fails to meet their desired objective or established benchmark. One optimal course of action is to refrain from striving for perfection. Acknowledge the veracity of the statement. Similar to individuals in general, you are not devoid of imperfections. The occurrence of errors is evident in your work.

Avoid being overly critical of oneself. Pardon. Cultivate a sense of self-compassion. This approach represents an expedient method to mitigate stress prior to its potential detrimental effects.

The Topic Of Interest Pertains To Familial Relationships.

Familial relationships encompass the various connections individuals establish with their immediate and extended family members. The term "family" encompasses a wide range of meanings and interpretations. Individuals frequently own their own unique interpretation of the concept of family. The concept of family varies depending on an individual's cultural, economic, and social context. Nevertheless, a basic characteristic shared by all families is that individuals who refer to others as "family" are expressing the significance of those individuals in their lives, so acknowledging them as integral members of their own family unit.

The concept of family can be defined as a fundamental social unit within a given civilization, often comprising of one or two parental figures and their offspring.

While the above definition serves as a suitable starting point, it fails to encompass several contemporary family arrangements that deviate from its parameters. Contemporary family structures encompass diverse arrangements, such as childless couples and other non-traditional configurations. An alternative interpretation of the concept of family pertains to a collective of two or more individuals who exhibit shared objectives and principles, exhibit enduring commitments towards each other, and typically cohabit within the same residence. This concept provides a more comprehensive representation of the bulk of contemporary family structures. In the course of this literary work, we shall employ the following definition as a means of establishing a connection with the subjects that will be addressed.

What are the defining characteristics that constitute a family unit? The conventional structure of a family typically comprises a female parent, a male parent, and their offspring. This particular family archetype is commonly shown in television shows and films. Nevertheless, in contemporary society, families are shown in a myriad of diverse forms that deviate significantly from the conventional model commonly envisioned by the majority. Currently, a significant number of children are raised in households headed by a lone parent, grandparents, or parents of the same gender. Certain families opt not to procreate or face limitations in doing so as a result of medical or emotional factors. The notion that a family consists of two parents and their offspring is the fundamental and rudimentary interpretation of the concept. In order to enhance our comprehension of familial connections, it is imperative to adopt a more expansive and inclusive definition. Furthermore, apart from the aforementioned broad interpretation, a significant number of individuals in contemporary culture perceive their friends as akin to family members or their pets as part of their familial unit.

The topic of interest pertains to the dynamics and interactions within professional relationships.

A professional relationship exhibits notable distinctions from the intimate relationships previously discussed, such as friendships and familial partnerships. A professional relationship can be defined as a continuous and dynamic connection between two individuals who adhere to predetermined boundaries that are considered suitable according to the standards set by their regulating bodies. The cultivation of professional relationships is fundamental to an individual's career advancement.

Professional partnerships encompass a diverse array of sorts. One commonly contemplated aspect is the interpersonal dynamic between individuals and their immediate supervisor or superior. If one assumes the role of a manager or boss, professional relationships primarily encompass the interactions and connections established with employees. Nevertheless, professional partnerships encompass a broader range of sorts than the aforementioned. Consider the dynamics of various professional connections, such as the association between a physician and a patient, an attorney and a client, an educator and a student, a service provider and a customer, among others. Professional relationships operate in a distinct manner compared to friendships and familial relationships. While maintaining a certain level of cordiality is important in most professional interactions, it is uncommon for individuals to perceive their doctor as a personal acquaintance.

Romantic relationships, also known as intimate relationships, are a fundamental aspect of human social interactions. These relationships involve emotional and sexual intimacy
Romantic interactions are prominently shown across various forms of media. As

we discussed previously, this form of relationship in western civilization carries more significance than other relationships. Conventional romantic partnerships typically involve individuals of opposite genders. Despite its antiquated nature, contemporary discourse characterises romantic relationships as a mutual agreement between two individuals to engage solely in a partnership imbued with passionate affection. In our modern-day, these partnerships can exist between a man and a woman, a man and a man, a woman and a woman, and other gender structure variants.

On top of that, there are also numerous forms of romantic partnerships. Love isn't one-size-fits-all. It implies something different to every single person, but it also feels and looks different to everyone. It is for this reason why there are so many distinct forms of romantic partnerships. These broadened definitions allow any person to find the ideal suit for their personality, lifestyle, and love concept.

Strategies For Stress Management Through Self-Help

The concept of stress refers to a psychological and physiological response that occurs when individuals perceive a discrepancy between the demands placed upon them and their ability to cope with those demands. Stress can be defined as a psychological and emotional condition characterized by heightened strain or tension, which arises as a consequence of challenging or unfavorable situations. When in this particular state, individuals experience a heightened perception of several imperative tasks that require immediate attention, despite the limited availability of necessary resources. The occurrence of strain or tension can be attributed to several external sources, such as disease, work-related demands, domestic circumstances, and familial situations. Interestingly, it is worth noting that even ostensibly joyous occasions such as holidays can sometimes give rise to feelings of stress.

The management of stress is beneficial due to its positive impact on individuals. The experience of stress can exert a significant influence on an individual's life, leading to feelings of sadness and therefore diminishing their level of productivity. The impact of this phenomenon on one's emotional stability is significant, since it also restricts cognitive functioning and impairs logical reasoning. Consequently, the implementation of efficient stress management techniques can significantly alleviate a substantial psychological and emotional load.

How can one ascertain their state of stress? This sort of mental pressure is accompanied by a range of ideas, emotions, bodily sensations, and behaviors. Several examples of these include:

The following are my reflections and considerations on the matter at hand.

I am unlikely to achieve this.

The situation lacks fairness. Assistance should be provided to me.
The current situation is overwhelming for me.
The topic of emotions is a subject of great interest and study in various academic disciplines. Em
Experiencing intense anger.
Experiencing symptoms of depression.
The individual expresses a sense of despair or lack of optimism.
The individual exhibits a lack of patience.
The topic of discussion pertains to physical sensations.
A physical sensation refers to a bodily reaction triggered by stress, which can be attributed to the release of adrenaline in the body. Certain physical sensations are commonly linked to the experience of stress.
The individual is exhibiting an increased respiratory rate.
The individual is experiencing elevated body temperature and perspiration.
The individual exhibits a state of restlessness.

Gastrointestinal issues, typically characterized by brief episodes of discomfort.

The challenge of maintaining concentration due to the diversion of one's attention.

The individual is experiencing a sensation of discomfort or pain in the head region, commonly referred to as a headache.

The subject of interest pertains to human behavior.

The phenomenon of insufficient sleep

The phenomenon of reduced desire to eat

It is not possible to reach a resolution.

The utilization of substances, specifically narcotics, or the escalation in their consumption. For instance, individuals who have developed a habitual smoking behavior are more likely to exhibit an elevated inclination towards engaging in smoking activities.

Engaging in Constructive Transformations

The primary objective of this intervention is to effectively regulate an individual's stress levels. Several steps can be implemented to effect constructive transformations. The aforementioned items encompass:

Please identify the sources of stress or pressures in your life.

Initiating this action represents the initial stride in effecting a constructive transformation. The execution of this stage is not as linear as it may initially appear. Identifying the origin of chronic stress can be a complex endeavor. In order to facilitate the process, the following inquiries may be employed to ascertain the underlying factors contributing to stress.

What are the factors that contribute to your experience of stress?

In what location do individuals typically find themselves when experiencing stress?

What is the nature of one's behavior during periods of stress?

With whom do I find myself in the company of when experiencing stress?

What modifications may I implement?

It may be observed that individuals may perceive limited agency in effecting change in certain circumstances. These minute actions has the potential to provide the desired outcome, hence it is advisable to execute them without delay. The elements that perpetuate the problem shall be identified.

After the identification of stress causes, the subsequent step involves identifying the perpetuating variables that contribute to the persistence of this issue.

Engaging in divergent thinking

This particular stage is primarily cognitive in nature. This implies that the only necessary adjustment is one's cognitive approach to different circumstances. In order to enhance cognitive abilities, it is advisable to consider a set of inquiries that one should pose when confronted with a specific scenario:

To what am I reacting?

What is the anticipated occurrence in this context?

Can this statement be classified as a fact or an opinion?

To what extent does adopting this cognitive approach contribute to one's overall effectiveness and success?

Is the endeavor deemed to be of sufficient value or merit?

Is there a possibility that I am overestimating the level of threat?

What interpretation am I ascribing to this particular circumstance?

Can an alternative perspective be considered in this context?

What recommendations could be offered to an individual facing a similar circumstance?

Is it possible to approach this situation in a manner that deviates from the conventional approach?

Upon engaging in introspection and providing candid responses to these inquiries, individuals will subsequently be capable of cultivating a constructive mindset towards a certain circumstance.

Engaging in alternative approaches

This measure will aid in the reduction of both tension and anxiety. What is the rationale behind this request? During periods of stress, individuals often experience a sense of being unable to meet many demands due to limited available resources. Hence, adopting alternative approaches, such as prioritizing essential apps, can contribute to the mitigation of stress levels.

Conversely, adopting alternative approaches can contribute to the mitigation of anxiety by enabling individuals to allocate dedicated periods each day for self-care and leisure activities. One may opt to establish a harmonious equilibrium, wherein sufficient time is allocated for work, leisure, and personal pursuits.

Neurotransmitters such as dopamine and serotonin serve as chemical messengers that transmit signals to various regions of the human body. The neural signals are subsequently received by the various regions of the brain, thereby enabling an individual to perceive and identify the objects or situations in their immediate environment. The neural signals transmitted to the brain also facilitate individuals in attributing emotional significance to their visual perceptions and experiences, thereby aiding in their behavioral responses and decision-making processes.

The limbic system is positioned anatomically beneath the cerebrum, which is considered the largest and most prominent region of the brain. The limbic system comprises various structures, such as the hippocampus, amygdala, and hypothalamus.

The amygdala serves as the central hub for the assignment of emotional significance to individual memories and events encountered by an individual.

Numerous studies have demonstrated that individuals or animals with amygdala impairments exhibit peculiar behavioral patterns. These manifestations can encompass an increase in sexual behavior, irrationality, aggression, or fearlessness.

The occurrence of Kluver-Bucy Syndrome, a rare disorder, has been documented in individuals who have suffered amygdala damage as a result of brain inflammation. The syndrome results in an altered emotional response to fear and anger, as well as difficulties in visual object recognition. Dementia and seizures represent two additional prominent symptoms associated with the syndrome.

The hippocampus is a neuroanatomical structure within the brain that plays a crucial role in facilitating the recall and execution of appropriate behavioral responses that align with an individual's current emotional state. As an illustration, when an individual experiences a state of happiness, they may be inclined to engage in a physical activity such as strolling within a park setting, thereby enabling them to derive pleasure from their environment. In the event that an individual experiences a state of emotional distress, they may opt to visit a bar where they are aware that the musical selection aligns with their prevailing mood.

Research has demonstrated that individuals experiencing chronic stress may exhibit a reduction in the size of their hippocampus. This explanation may shed light on certain characteristic aspects of depression, such as the presence of an ambiguous or indistinct recollection of personal memories.

The hypothalamus is a crucial region of the brain responsible for regulating the secretion of hormones that play a significant role in modulating an individual's mood and facilitating their survival. The hypothalamus is responsible for regulating autonomic functions such as respiration, cardiac activity, sleep patterns, and perspiration. The limbic system is responsible for regulating physiological processes that correspond to an individual's emotional and mood states, such as increased heart rate or muscle tension in response to feelings of frustration.

Given the primitive nature of the limbic system, it is observed that the day-to-day decision-making processes of individuals are predominantly influenced by the more recently evolved neural networks that regulate cognitive and behavioral responses in specific circumstances. The objective is for an individual's conduct to facilitate the attainment of their long-term objectives, rather than being solely influenced by their emotional state.

Despite the presence of various components within the limbic system that impact the alignment of behaviors with emotions, researchers continue to investigate the more recent networks in order to enhance their comprehension of how the brain regulates individuals' emotional states. The cognitive control network and the autobiographic memory network are the two specific systems that are currently under closer examination.

The cognitive control network facilitates interconnectivity among various brain regions, enabling the coordination of attention and concentration processes to effectively accomplish a given task. The present neural network within the brain engages the anterior region of the cingulate cortex and the dorsolateral prefrontal cortex. The aforementioned brain regions exhibit specialization in cognitive processes characterized by a lack of emotional influence and a propensity for rational thinking.

When Confronted With A Panic Attack, It Is Imperative To Engage In The Process Of Rewiring One's Brain.

When faced with a panic attack, it is recommended to implement the following four strategies in order to promptly alleviate distress and create mental capacity for constructive thoughts and emotions.

The initial step involves maintaining a state of mindfulness and directing one's attention towards identifying the potential underlying cause of the panic attack. It is imperative to observe the manner in which one's body perceives a threat that one is encountering or how it responds to the present circumstances. Attempt to direct your attention towards each individual emotion or cognitive process that you are experiencing.

Step 2: Release one's grasp on the subject matter. To sever the connection between the body and mind, one must engage in the practice of clearing the mind from judgments and thoughts. It is important to refrain from assigning blame to oneself or others for the occurrence of panic attacks. It is important to recognize that this occurrence is not limited solely to oneself, but can affect individuals across a broad spectrum.

Step 3 involves directing attention towards the remaining elements or aspects. Direct your attention towards the emotions and physical sensations that your body is experiencing. Does the individual experience any pain, tremors, or sensations of tightness in any specific area? Is the individual experiencing a condition in which they are incapable of physical movement or verbal communication? Direct your focus towards these sensations without attempting to alter or manipulate them. Proceed to the fourth step, which involves the act of inhaling and exhaling air, commonly referred to as breathing. Engage in a series of regular, uniform, seamless, and cadenced inhalations and exhalations. Engaging in this practice will assist individuals in achieving a state of inner balance and focus.

Step 5: Envision a feather eliciting favorable reactions. Please close your eyes and continue to engage in the act of respiration. Visualize a feather gently stimulating the outer layer of the amygdala through the power of mental imagery. In the event of initial failure, it is advisable to persist in one's efforts until a sensation akin to a gentle feather grazing the amygdala is experienced. This intervention can assist in alleviating the symptoms of anxiety or panic attacks and elicit various beneficial reactions within the brain.

In conclusion,

Anxiety disorders have the potential to induce a highly distressing state, wherein the individual may perceive the prospect of finding a resolution as insurmountable. The individual experiences a sense of confinement within a limited and constricting space, hindering their ability to lead a conventional lifestyle. Anxiety is also accompanied by physiological manifestations. In addition to inducing cardiac palpitations and muscular tension, it can also give rise to sleep disturbances and gastrointestinal issues. Given that individuals afflicted with anxiety disorders are prone to undermining their own well-being and achievements, it is imperative to assume complete mastery over this condition. The rapid pace and intensity of contemporary existence have engendered a perception that experiencing happiness and serenity are now regarded as indulgences, rather than integral components of everyday life. Anxiety disorders can induce a range of symptoms, including irritability, apprehension, impaired concentration, reduced productivity, fatigue, physical discomfort, and dizziness. Anxiety has the potential to significantly impact individuals' professional and personal lives, leading to detrimental effects on their careers and marriages, ultimately resulting in individuals becoming entrapped by their own ruminative cognitions.

Nevertheless, individuals have the capacity to perceive a sense of liberation and acquire expertise in leading a contented existence devoid of apprehension and episodes of intense fear. If an individual perceives themselves to be experiencing symptoms indicative of a severe anxiety disorder and finds that theaforementioned suggestions provided are insufficient in addressing their concerns, it is advisable to seek consultation with a psychotherapist to obtain additional assistance. It is important to acknowledge that one is not alone in their experiences and that there is no reason to feel ashamed.

Individuals possess inherent strength, worthiness, and deserve to lead a life devoid of anxiety. Individuals who experience difficulties related to panic attacks,anxiety, or fear should be assured that there is no inherent flaw or deficiency within them. The experience in question is an inherent component of one's existence that necessitates active management.

Effectively Regulate Emotional Responses

Many individuals were likely socialised to adhere to the belief that emotions should be suppressed or disregarded in certain contexts. It has been established that this approach is antiquated and no longer applicable in contemporary work contexts. The leader bears the obligation of comprehending and effectively handling the emotions present inside the discussion. Robert Plutchik, a former professor at the Albert Einstein College of Medicine, developed a comprehensive model known as the "wheel of emotions" to illustrate the sequential nature of emotional experiences. The initial experience of annoyance can progress to feelings of anger and, in severe instances, escalate to a state of wrath. One might mitigate this issue by demonstrating mindfulness towards upholding an individual's dignity and exhibiting respectful behaviour towards them, even in instances where there may be a divergence of opinions.

Developing an Ease with Silence

Instances may arise during the course of a conversation wherein a period of quiet ensues. It is advisable to use caution and refrain from hastily populating the text with excessive verbiage. Similar to how the interval between musical notes enhances our appreciation of the music, the intermittent moments of silence during a conversation serve to facilitate the comprehension of spoken words and enable the absorption of the conveyed message. In addition to its relaxing properties, a stop can facilitate improved interpersonal connections. For instance, those who identify as extroverts may experience discomfort at moments of quiet, since they are accustomed to engaging in verbal expression as a means of cognitive processing. The behaviour described can be interpreted as exhibiting dominance or assertiveness, particularly when interacting with others that possess introverted tendencies. Introverted individuals exhibit a preference for engaging in thoughtful reflection prior to verbalising their thoughts. Cease verbal communication and provide them the opportunity to express themselves, since it has the potential to result in a more favourable outcome.

Maintain the Relationship
A leader characterised by a high level of emotional intelligence consistently demonstrates mindfulness in minimising any potential negative consequences on interpersonal relationships. The process of establishing strong interpersonal connections necessitates a significant investment of time, spanning across several years, while the act of severing these connections can occur just a

matter of minutes. Consider the potential for dialogue to ameliorate the circumstances, while avoiding the creation of an insurmountable barrier in interpersonal relations.

It is vital to maintain consistency.

It is imperative to ensure that the purpose is equitable and that a uniform methodology is employed. For instance, if an individual perceives that you apply one set of rules for one person and a distinct set for another, you will be viewed as exhibiting favouritism. Perceived disparity can rapidly deteriorate a relationship. Employees possess enduring recollections of your past handling of events. Strive for coherence in your leadership methodology. A consistent leader instills trust among individuals as their unwavering stance on significant matters, such as culture, business principles, and acceptable behaviours, eliminates the need for speculation or doubt.

Enhancing One's Conflict Resolution Aptitude

Conflict is an inherent component of interpersonal engagement among individuals. The successful management of conflict is considered a crucial ability within the realm of leadership. Having a repertoire of well-established phrases might be advantageous in critical situations.

What Is The Recommended Method For Administering Medication?

In order to achieve optimal efficacy, it is necessary to adhere to a regular dosing regimen of antidepressant medication for a minimum duration of four to six weeks. It is imperative to maintain medication adherence even after experiencing symptom relief, as doing so can serve as a preventive measure against the recurrence of depression.

It is imperative to discontinue medicine alone under the careful guidance of a medical professional. It is often necessary to taper off the use of certain medications in order to provide the body sufficient time to acclimatise. Although antidepressants do not possess addictive properties or induce habit formation, abruptly discontinuing their use might result in the onset of withdrawal symptoms or, in more severe cases, a complete recurrence of depressive symptoms. A considerable number of individuals afflicted with chronic and persistent depression disorders may require ongoing medication for an indefinite duration.

Moreover, in the event that an individual discovers that a specific category of medication is ineffective, it is highly advisable to contemplate transitioning to an alternative medication. Research findings indicate that individuals who did not exhibit any discernible changes following treatment with a particular medicine demonstrated a heightened likelihood of recovering from depression upon initiating a different medication or augmenting their existing medication regimen.

In the event that an individual has any atypical or idiosyncratic side effects while undergoing antidepressant treatment, it is imperative to promptly communicate these symptoms to one's healthcare provider. Furthermore, it is recommended that individuals diligently observe and assess their symptoms upon initiating a novel pharmaceutical regimen. It is advisable to maintain a record of one's symptoms and monitor their progression, noting any improvements or exacerbations. The acquisition of more information enables individuals and their healthcare providers to refine pharmaceutical dosages in order to get the most favourable outcome.

Discovering One's Authentic Identity. The Process Of Emptying Out.!

Inhale and exhale air to facilitate respiration. Develop an awareness of the immediate environment. Observe the walls and take note of the artwork and colour schemes, as well as the substantial expanse of the area. The majority of rooms are primarily characterised by their spaciousness. Direct your gaze on my words. Please take note of the space that exists between the words and maintain a focus on your physical presence. During this process, it is helpful to conceptualise the mind as a container. Please clear the contents of the container, including your ideas, your sense of self, your list of tasks, your many roles, and any judgements or reactions. Recite the phrase, "Deplete one's thoughts. Deplete one's thoughts."

It is recommended to maintain bodily presence while keeping one's eyes open. It is acceptable if they decide to close. Please reopen them at your convenience.

It is important to be cognizant of one's environment. Develop a sense of gratitude and engage in a more profound exploration.

The command "freeze" is issued. Experience the sensory stimuli from the preceding exercise in a frozen state, while you descend further into a state of deep meditation. One must recall the state of heightened awareness characterised by a profound sense of tranquilly. Experience it. Upon the act of depleting the vessel, namely the corporeal being, one is ultimately left with one's own essence. The concept under discussion can be described as a "isness." The concept of pure awareness refers to a state of consciousness characterised by a heightened level of perception and understanding without the influence of external stimuli The concept of pure consciousness refers to a state of awareness devoid of any specific content or mental activity. It is important to acknowledge this. The concept being discussed is one's fundamental nature or core identity. It is important to recognise any thoughts that may come, but it is advisable to refrain from actively engaging with them. It is advised against accessing or logging onto them. The individual is metaphorically likened to the sky, while the clouds are used as a representation of transient thoughts.

Respire. Direct your attention to the act of breathing. Consider a hypothetical scenario in which an individual's cardiac organ is intricately linked to a symbolically significant jade pearl of affection situated at the core of the planet Earth. Upon inhalation, one experiences the sensation of affection intensifying, accompanied by a sensation of heat emanating from the palms of the hands and a tingling sensation in the fingertips. When exhaling, individuals express affirmation towards existence, symbolised by the utterance of "YES," while simultaneously experiencing the opening of their metaphorical heart doors. One experiences a profound sensation of love as intense vibrations stimulate each particle of the body, evoking an overwhelming sense of unconditional affection.

5) Recognise the sensation of the heart and brain establishing a connection. Experience the palpable tranquilly. The sensation might be likened to a state in which the entirety of one's physical being is expressing a sense of joy or contentment. The term "Buddha nature" refers to the concept articulated by Buddha.

The Potential Hazards Linked To Micro Dosing

Despite an optimistic perspective, microdosing is typically seen as a safe practise; yet, it does have certain hazards. The symptoms encompass a spectrum of cognitive challenges, such as diminished ability to focus, as well as unanticipated manifestations, like heightened levels of anxiety and physiological unease.

Individuals who have received a diagnosis of psychotic disorders, such as schizophrenia or bipolar disorder, are advised against the use of psychedelic substances at any level of dosage due to the potential occurrence of adverse outcomes. The phenomenon of microdosing has been seen to potentially elevate neuroticism levels, as indicated by a single study relying on self-reported data. However, it is important to note that these findings have yet to be substantiated by rigorous clinical studies. In the context of the aforementioned discourse, James Fadiman highlighted three specific aspects pertaining to the subject matter during his conversation with Sam Harris. Currently, there exists a dearth of scholarly investigations pertaining to the effects of psychedelics on individuals diagnosed with schizophrenia or bipolar disorders. This scarcity can be attributed to the perceived risks associated with administering such substances, which have deterred researchers from undertaking comprehensive studies in this area. Conversely, a substantial volume of anecdotal evidence has been amassed from individuals with bipolar disorder who have self-reported their personal experiences with psychedelics. Thirdly, those who have provided accounts often assert that employing these substances during a manic state is ill-advised, whereas pleasant encounters have been documented during a sad state.

Engaging in comprehensive research prior to combining any medications, especially frequently consumed prescription pharmaceuticals, is consistently advisable. It is strongly advised that those who are now using antidepressant drugs seek consultation from a psychiatrist before engaging in microdosing practises. Microdosing is contraindicated for individuals with colour vision deficiency, chronic anxiety disorders, or those diagnosed with autism spectrum disorder.

When contemplating the use of psychedelic substances in any manifestation, it is imperative to do a thorough examination of the material to ascertain its level of purity. In instances where psychedelic substances are consumed in non-clinical environments, there exists the potential for the presence of adulterants that may pose significant health risks. Harm-reduction networks provide access to testing kits that can be utilised to determine the purity of substances.

The Present Discourse Concerns The Topic Of Panic Disorder And Agoraphobia.

Panic disorder is distinguished by the occurrence of recurrent panic attacks. A panic attack is an abrupt manifestation of fear response that appears to occur spontaneously. In essence, the observed phenomenon can be characterised as a fear response in the absence of any discernible threat. When confronted with a situation that poses a significant threat to one's life, it is inevitable to undergo a sense of terror. However, it is crucial to acknowledge that this anxiety is rational and fitting in such circumstances. When individuals experience an inexplicable manifestation of heightened terror, it is frequently seen that they may envision themselves succumbing to mortality or losing their mental faculties.

While panic attacks are a characteristic feature of panic disorder, it is important to note that the presence of panic attacks alone does not constitute a diagnosis of panic disorder. There exists a subset of individuals who have panic attacks without progressing to the clinical diagnosis of panic disorder. In order to meet the criteria for a diagnosis of panic disorder, it is necessary for an individual to experience heightened levels of anxiety in relation to panic attacks, as well as maintain a belief that further panic episodes are likely to transpire. The apprehension around prospective episodes of panic frequently motivates individuals with agoraphobia to engage in avoidance behaviours. Agoraphobia manifests when an individual engages in avoidance behaviours or expeditiously exits from circumstances that elicit heightened anxiety, potentially leading to a panic attack. Panic disorder is characterised by the occurrence of disruptive panic attacks. However, it is worth noting that the most significant disruption associated with this illness generally stems from agoraphobic avoidance. As one delves into the subject matter, it becomes evident that agoraphobic avoidance can manifest in such a profound manner that the affected individual may find themselves confined to their residence, incapable of engaging in employment beyond the confines of their domestic environment, and unable to maintain a typical social existence.

The fight-or-flight response, sometimes known as the fight-or-flight syndrome, is a physiological reaction that occurs in response to a perceived

The fight-or-flight syndrome has been previously addressed, therefore establishing familiarity with its nature as the physiological reaction of the body to a circumstance perceived as potentially life-threatening. This syndrome refers to the physiological response of the body in anticipation of engaging in either a flight response to evade danger or a fight response to defend oneself in a life-threatening situation. The often used term "fight-or-flight syndrome" might be more logically expressed as "flight-or-fight" when considering its conceptual framework. The rationale behind the act of reversing this behaviour lies in the inherent desire to prioritise escape above engaging in combat, reserving the latter as a last resort when no avenue for escape is feasible. It is plausible that at a certain juncture in one's existence, an individual may have received cautionary advice regarding the potential hazards associated with confining an animal to a cornered position. When an animal is confined to a corner, it is likely to perceive a threat to its existence and respond accordingly by preparing to engage in a fight until its demise, assuming there are no available means of escape. In the event that the animal in question is of diminutive size, it is highly probable that its capacity to inflict harm against a human as a prospective predator is negligible. However, it is important to acknowledge that during a confrontation of utmost significance, the aforementioned animal might indeed cause harm.

The fight-or-flight response is considered to be one of the first evolutionary adaptations in humans. The activation of this physiological response occurs within the brainstem, specifically within a region referred to as the locus coeruleus. The syndrome is not exclusive to the human species. The presence of a brainstem is observed in nearly all organisms possessing a brain, as even organisms with rudimentary brains have this anatomical structure. The observation that the response in

question emerged early in the process of evolution and has been conserved across a wide range of species implies its significant role in promoting survival.

Panic episodes can be characterised as terror responses; yet, they are often perceived as false alarms. The brain perpetually engages in the analysis of environmental stimuli, and when seeing potential threats, initiates the fight-or-flight response. However, in the absence of any perceived threat, we find ourselves perplexed by our panic reaction. The brain has erroneously concluded the presence of danger, leading to this response despite the absence of any actual risk. Every living organism or inanimate entity that is engineered to react to various circumstances possesses the inherent capacity to exhibit erroneous responses. It is assumed that the audience possesses a certain level of familiarity with smoke detectors. These devices are specifically engineered to extract a limited segment of the surrounding environment, specifically targeting substances like smoke. Upon detecting a sufficient quantity of smoke-like material, they emit a highly audible alert to indicate the potential presence of a fire. Please observe and identify all the qualifying words present in the above phrase. It is widely acknowledged that smoke detectors may intermittently activate in the absence of an actual fire, hence exemplifying a false alarm. It is possible that an item may have been inadvertently incinerated in the oven or that an alarm may have been triggered when boiling water. In the event of such an occurrence, the smoke detector is either reset or its battery is temporarily removed.

However, the human brain exhibits a significantly higher level of complexity compared to a smoke detector. The ability to reset or deactivate the brain's functioning is not feasible when confronted with the occurrence of a panic attack, which is characterised by a false alarm response. In contrast, the human brain endeavours to discern the nature and causality of observed phenomena. The most salient aspects of the current situation are the distressing encounters that appear to lack justification from our perspective. However, it seems improbable that other organisms, such as rats, possess an equivalent perception of the fight-or-flight response. It is probable that their cognitive abilities are insufficient to comprehend and experience such emotional states. However, these organisms exhibit the cognitive ability to stimulate their physiological systems in order to engage in evasive manoeuvres or engage in combat as a means of ensuring their survival. It is plausible that a significant portion of our emotional repertoire had its origins in less cognitively advanced organisms, so implying that the subjective experience of these emotions in such organisms may differ from our own. The advancement of our brain's growth has facilitated our capacity to engage in cognitive processes, enabling us to analyse and comprehend the external environment as well as internal bodily sensations.

www.ingramcontent.com/pod-product-compliance
Lightning Source LLC
Chambersburg PA
CBHW052143110526
44591CB00012B/1842